HATCH!

by Karyn Henley
pictures by
Susan Kennedy

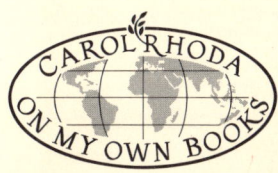

Carolrhoda Books • Minneapolis, Minnesota

Copyright © 1980 by CAROLRHODA BOOKS, INC.

All rights reserved. International copyright secured. Manufactured in the United States of America. Published simultaneously in Canada by J. M. Dent & Sons (Canada) Ltd., Don Mills, Ontario.

LIBRARY OF CONGRESS CATALOGING IN PUBLICATION DATA

Henley, Karyn.
Hatch!

(On my own books)
SUMMARY: Briefly describes the nesting habits of such diverse egg-laying creatures as the whale shark, Siamese fighting fish, grasshopper, emperor penguin, ostrich, duckbilled platypus, and others.

1. Parental behavior in animals—Juvenile literature. 2. Animals, Infancy of—Juvenile literature. 3. Reproduction—Juvenile literature. [1. Eggs. 2. Parental behavior in animals. 3. Animals—Infancy. 4. Reproduction] I. Kennedy, Susan. II. Title.

QL762.H46   1980   591.5'6   79-91306
ISBN 0-87614-122-X lib. bdg.

1 2 3 4 5 6 7 8 9 10 85 84 83 82 81 80

With love to Raygan
—K. H.

To Mom, Dad, Bill, Carol, Pete, and Ross
—S. K.

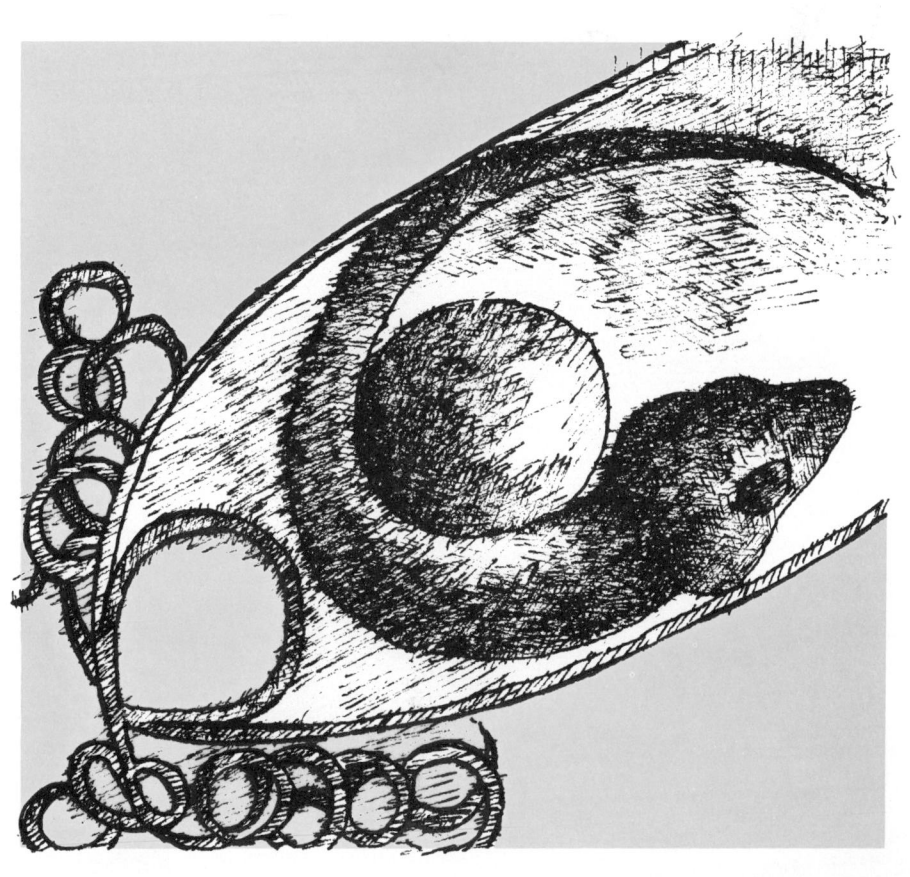

Deep in the sea is a soft, brown case.

It is called a Mermaid's Purse.

But it does not belong to a mermaid.

It belongs to a Whale Shark.

A baby is growing inside.

The case is its egg shell.

Like Whale Sharks,
many animals begin their lives
inside eggs.
Here is a list of them.

birds	lizards
frogs	turtles
toads	crocodiles
salamanders	alligators
insects	most fishes
spiders	most snakes
Spiny Anteaters	Duckbill Platypuses

Eggs come in all sizes.

Some are tiny.

Look at the nail on your little finger.

Hummingbird eggs are about that size.

Frog eggs are even smaller.

Other eggs are large.

Ostrich eggs are eight inches long.

They weigh three pounds!

But no matter what size the egg is
it has a nest just right for it.

The Siamese Fighting Fish
has an unusual nest.
The father makes it.
It is a bubble nest.
It floats at the top of the water.
The mother lays her eggs.
Father catches them in his mouth.
He blows them into the nest.
Then he chases mother away.
She leaves.
But father stays.
He watches the nest.
He keeps it safe.

Finally the babies hatch.
But they can not swim yet.
They must stay in the nest
for three more days.
Sometimes a baby falls out.
Then the father hurries to it.
He takes it in his mouth.
He blows it back into the nest.

Spiders also hatch from eggs.
First the mother makes an egg case.
It is called a cocoon.
She fills it with eggs.
Then she puts it in a safe place.

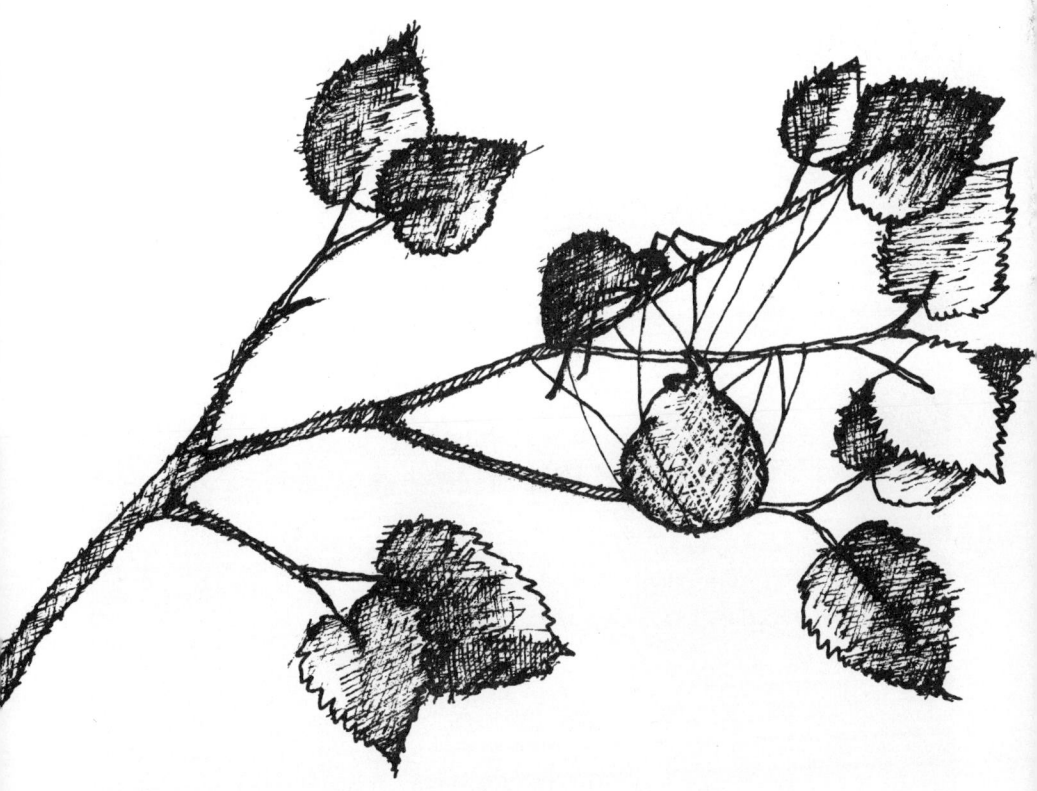

Mother Wolf Spider
has a very safe place
for her cocoon.
She carries it underneath her.
Soon the babies hatch.
Then they ride on her back.
They stay there for several days.
Then they are on their own.

The babies face many dangers.
Frogs and birds like to eat them.
Bad weather can kill them.
Sometimes there is not enough
for them to eat.
One hundred spiders may hatch.
But only two may live to grow up.

Grasshopper eggs also need a safe place.
So mother grasshopper hides her nest.
She makes a tunnel in the ground.
She lays her eggs there.

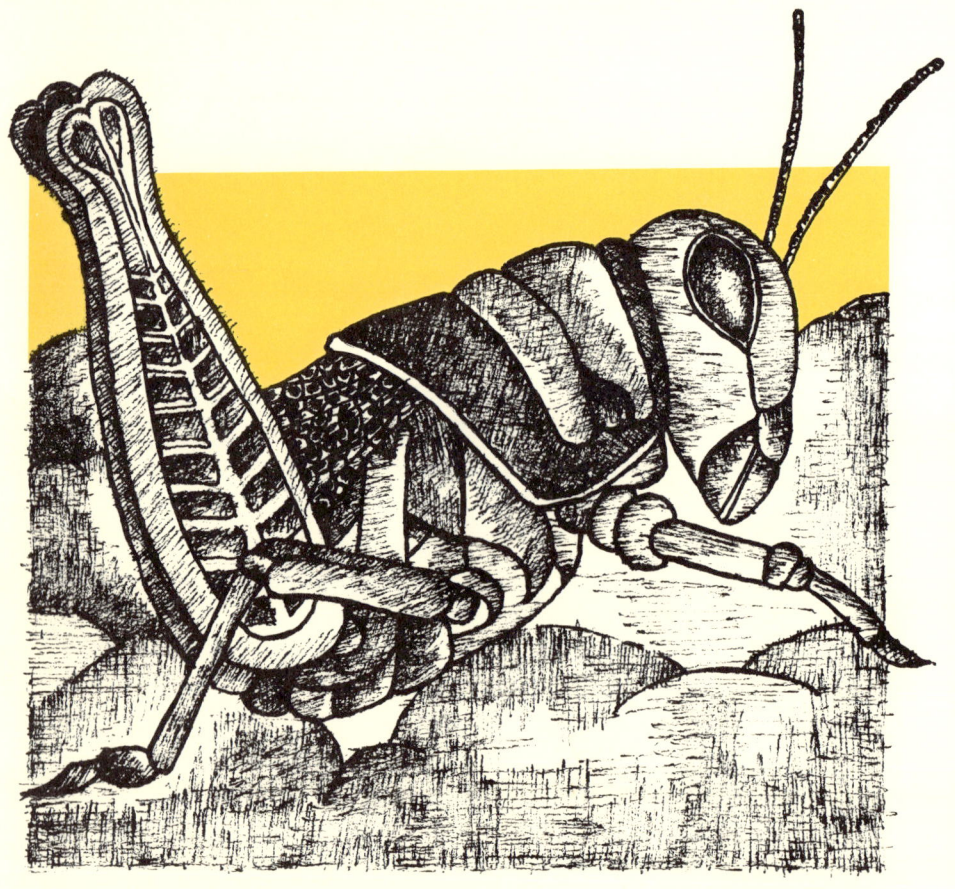

The eggs look a little like rice.
They are inside a case.
It's called an egg pod.
Mother lays them in the fall.
Then she leaves them alone.
They will stay safe in their nest all winter.
They will hatch in the spring.

Turtles dig holes for their eggs too.
Mother digs a hole in the ground.
Or she may dig it in wet sand.
She lays her eggs.
Then she leaves them alone.
Her babies do not need her.
But they do need heat.
The sun will keep them warm.
They also need to be kept damp.
So turtle egg shells are soft.
A little water from the damp nest gets through the soft shells.

Soon the babies hatch.
They can take care of themselves right away.

Most snakes also lay eggs.
Snake eggs do not need any help
from their parents either.
Mother lays them in the damp ground.
Then she can leave them alone.
Like turtles, the new baby snakes
can take care of themselves.

The Midwife Toad has a funny nest.
Mother lays a string of eggs.
It can be four feet long.
There may be 60 to 70 eggs
in the string.
Then father takes the string of eggs.
He twists it around his back legs.
He will carry it there
until the eggs hatch.

When the babies hatch,
they do not look like toads.
They are round.
They have long tails.
They do not have legs.

They look like little fish.
The babies are called
tadpoles or polliwogs.
Later they will grow legs.
And their tails will disappear.

Mother Surinam Toad
lays about 100 eggs.
Their nest is on her back.
Each egg sits in a pocket in her skin.
Inside a tadpole is growing.
The eggs are ready to hatch
in about ten weeks.
But the babies are not tadpoles
anymore.
They are little toads now.
Off they hop.
They will not need their mother.
They are on their own.

Most people have seen a bird's nest.
But not all birds make nests.
Emperor Penguins live in Antarctica.
It is very cold there.
The ground is covered with ice.
There are no trees or bushes.
There is nothing with which
to build a nest.
Father takes care of the egg.
Its "nest" is on top of his feet!

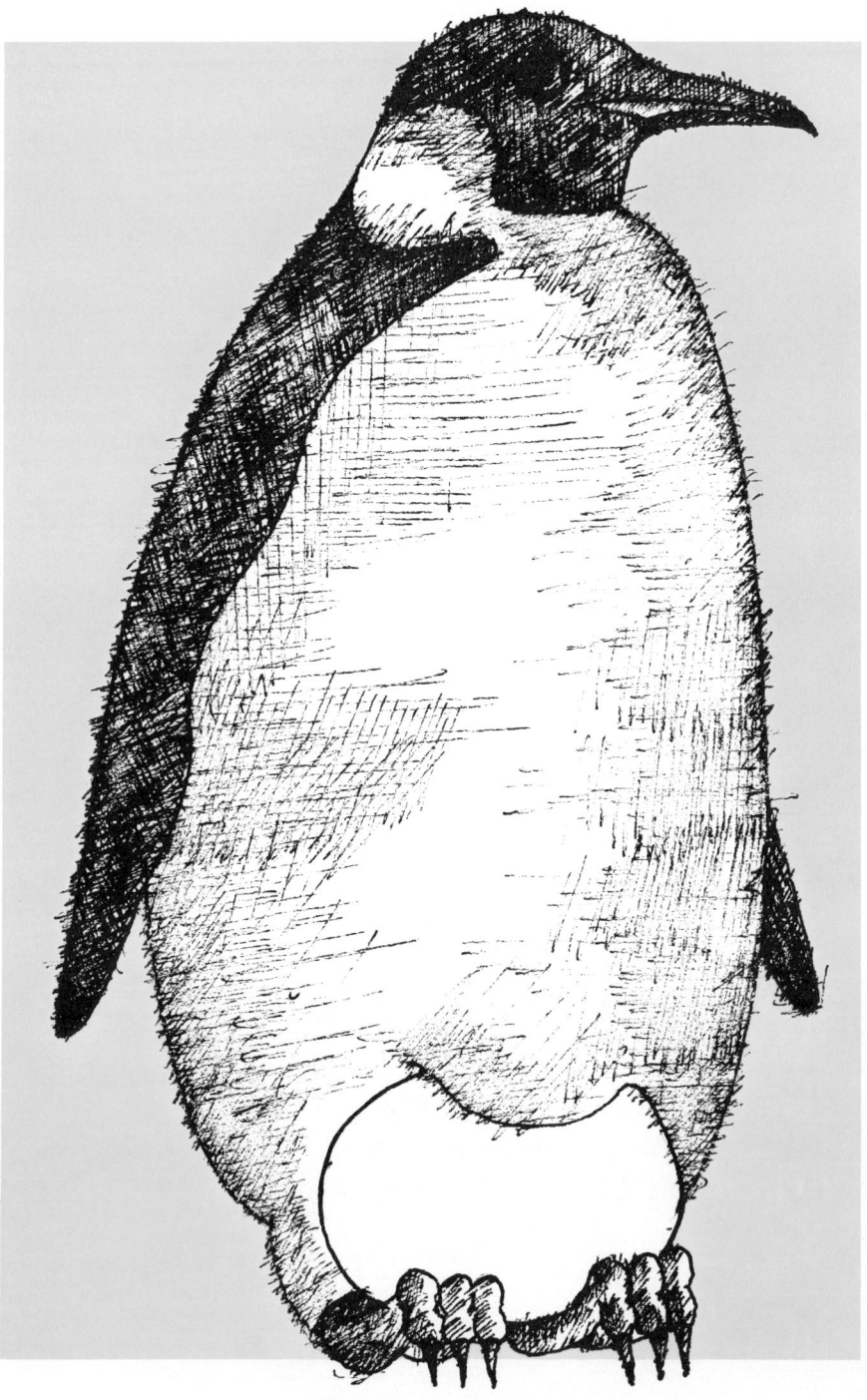

The egg is five inches long.

It sits on father's feet.

He covers it with a fold of his skin.

That keeps the egg nice and warm.

Of course, father can not walk very far.

If he did, the egg might break.

He holds the egg for two months.
He can not move around.
So he can not hunt for food.
He does not eat.
He stays with the other fathers.
They stand close together to keep warm.

Finally the baby is ready to hatch.
Now mother comes back.
She has been away all this time.
She has been eating.
Now it is father's turn to eat.
It is mother's turn to take the egg.
The egg hatches on her feet.
While the baby is little,
it stays on mother's feet.
It is warm there.
And the baby gets a free ride.

Cuckoo birds do not make nests either.
They do not take care
of their babies at all.
Instead, a cuckoo mother
watches other birds.
She waits for one to leave her nest.
Then she quickly lays her egg
in the other bird's nest.
And then she flies away.

Cuckoo babies are not very nice.
They hatch before the other eggs.
Then they push the other eggs
out of the nest.
They do not want to share their food
with other babies.

Ostriches have big families.
There are three mothers and one father.
They have 15 to 20 babies.
The mothers all lay their eggs
in the same nest.
The nest is a hole in the ground.
The father made it.
He sits on the eggs at night.
One of the mothers sits on them
during the day.

After 40 to 45 days

the babies are ready to hatch.

They sing inside their eggs.

Their parents call back.

The babies learn their parents' voices before they are born!
They will stay with their parents for a whole year.

Baby alligators also tell their parent when they are hatching.
They make high barking cries.

They are calling their mother.
They need her help
to get out of their nest!

Mother alligator made the nest.
She piled up mud and grass.
She made a hole for the eggs
at the top of the pile.
She laid 40 to 60 eggs there.
Then she covered the hole.
For two months she stayed near by.
Now her babies are calling her.
They are hatching.
She hurries to dig them out.

The Duckbill Platypus
also covers its nest.
Platypuses live in dens in the ground.
When it is time to lay her eggs,
mother digs a new room.

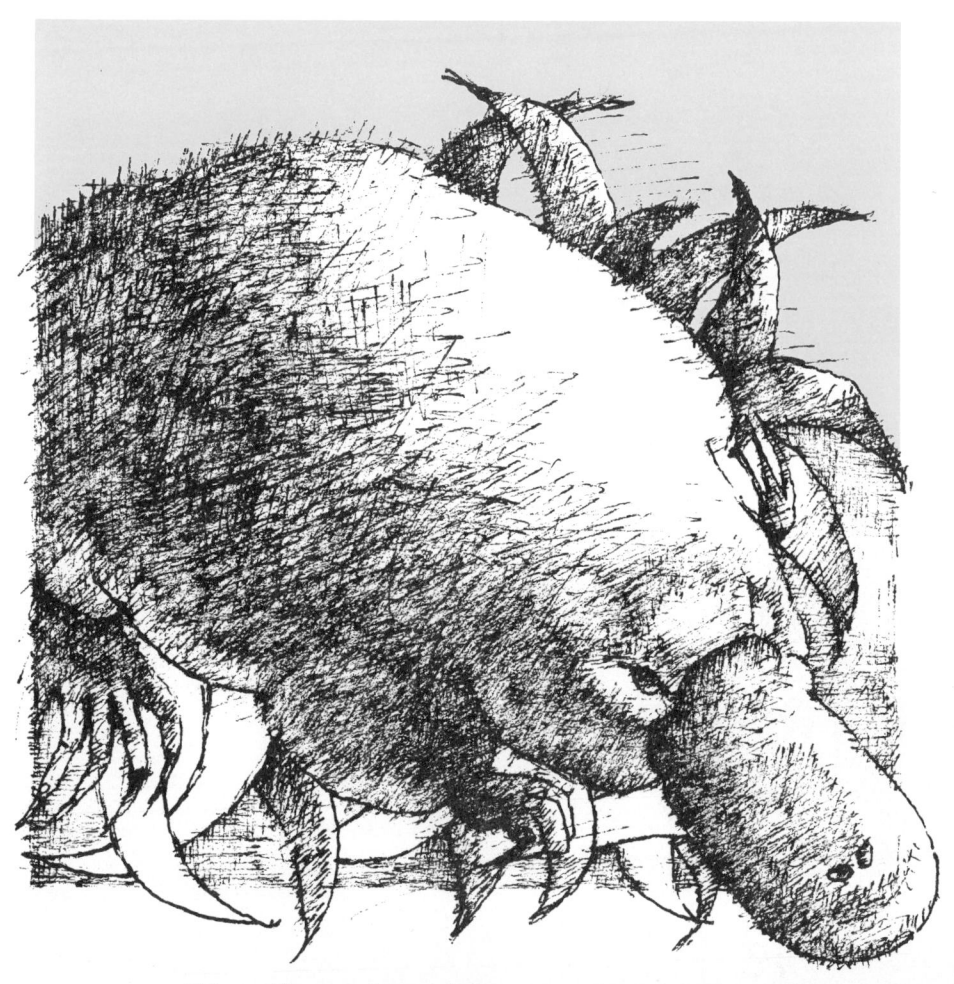

She lines it with wet leaves.
These will keep her eggs
from drying up.
Then she shuts herself inside.
She lays two soft eggs.

Her babies will hatch in 12 days.
But they are helpless.
They can not see yet.
They must stay inside the den
for about 17 weeks.
Mother feeds them milk.
It comes from tiny holes in her tummy.
The babies lick the milk off her hair.

These are just some of the animals
that hatch from eggs.
Each one lays its own special eggs.
Each takes care of them
in its own special way.
Each egg has a nest
just right for it.
There it sits and waits.
And one day—
pecking, pushing, and shoving—
a tiny animal hatches
into a bright new world.